Juices

Apple

Banana

Beetroot

Blackcurrant

Carrot

Celery

Cherry

Coconut water

Grape

Guava

Kiwi

Lemon

Mango

Orange

Papaya

Pear

Pineapple

Pomegranate

Strawberry

Sugarcane

Tamarind

Tomato

Watermelon

www.ingramcontent.com/pod-product-compliance
Lightning Source LLC
Chambersburg PA
CBHW041526070526
44585CB00002B/99